QUESTIO

Wooden Boat Construction

Ron Jurd

Newnes Technical Books

The Butterworth Group

United Kingdom   **Butterworth & Co (Publishers) Ltd**
London: 88 Kingsway, WC2B 6AB

Australia   **Butterworths Pty Ltd**
Sydney: 586 Pacific Highway, NSW 2067
Also at Melbourne, Brisbane, Adelaide and Perth

Canada   **Butterworth & Co (Canada) Ltd**
Toronto: 2265 Midland Avenue, Scarborough,
Ontario, M1P 4S1

New Zealand   **Butterworths of New Zealand Ltd**
Wellington: T & W Young Building,
77—85 Customhouse Quay, 1 CPO Box 472

South Africa   **Butterworth & Co (South Africa) (Pty) Ltd**
Durban: 152—154 Gale Street

USA   **Butterworth (Publishers) Inc**
Boston: 19 Cummings Park, Woburn, Mass. 01801

First published 1978 by Newnes Technical Books
a Butterworth imprint

© Butterworth & Co (Publishers) Ltd, 1978

British Library Cataloguing in Publication Data

Jurd, Ron
    Questions and answers on wooden boat construction
    1. Boat-building — Amateurs' manuals
    I. Title
    623.82'07'4   VM351   78-40011

    ISBN 0 408 00315 4

Typeset by Butterworths Litho-Preparation Department
Printed in England by Cox & Wyman Ltd.,
London, Fakenham and Reading

PREFACE

This book will be of practical help and guidance to boatbuilding apprentices, the amateur constructor, model makers, etc, who are interested or involved in the building of wooden boats.

Although not intended as a complete treatise on the subject of wooden boatbuilding, it covers most of the everyday problems which confront the boatbuilder. Numerous drawings are included to help with the interpretation of the text.

The author gratefully acknowledges the British Standards Institution for the information on adhesives and plywood; Lloyds Register of Shipping for quotations from the Lloyds Rules for Building Wooden Boats, and Borden Chemicals for information on adhesives.

Ron Jurd

CONTENTS

1

TYPES OF CONSTRUCTION

Which are the main types of wooden boat construction in use today?

Carvel, Clencher or Lapstrake, Double diagonal, Strip planking.

What are the characteristics of carvel construction?

The planking of a carvel build boat is laid, or fitted, fore and aft, each plank or strake being fitted edge to edge with the next. This gives a smooth appearance to the hull.

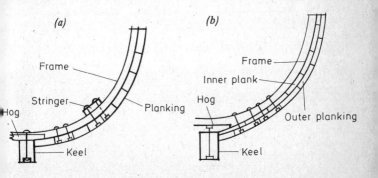

Fig. 1. (a) Section of single planked carvel hull. (b) Section of double skin carvel hull

The planking is secured to frames which may be grown, bent, or, in the case of composite construction, of metal. The fastenings may be of wood (treenails), screws, copper nails and roves, ring barbed nails, iron nails (dumps), or bolts (*Fig. 1a*).

The seams may be caulked and stopped, splined or even close fitted.

Occasionally double skin planking is used, in this case the plank edges are staggered, e.g. spaced one half plank width alternately, so that they appear as (*Fig. 1b*).

It is usual for this type of planking to have a membrane of oiled cloth or other suitable material between the layers of planking.

Describe clencher (clinker) or lapstrake construction

This is a very popular method of construction, particularly for small craft such as dinghies and fishing boats. A number of class boats of larger size such as the Folkboat and the Stella are built in this way (*Fig. 2a*).

Clencher is one of the oldest known methods of building and there are examples of Viking and Norse ships still in

Fig. 2(a) A clencher dinghy

existence. In clencher construction the planking is laid, or fitted, so that the edge of each strake or plank overlaps the next and a section of its face is fastened to its neighbour. This gives the craft a stepped or joggled appearance (*Fig. 2b*).

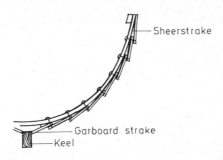

Fig. 2(b) A clencher hull section

In the case of the conventional clencher boat, the planking is fastened to frames or timbers, which may be grown (sawn) or bent, the planks being fastened together and to the timbers or frames with nails which are either roved and clenched or turned.

A method also in use today is glued ply clencher, the strakes are glued to each other at the lands to make a similar finish to the conventional type. It is not usual to fit timbers or frames to these boats as this makes the boat unsuitable for the rough usage which the average dinghy or tender has to cope with.

Clencher is a very strong construction due to the way that each plank overlaps its neighbour. This forms, in effect, a double thickness longitudinal stringer. It is easy to repair, but has the disadvantage that leaks at the seams can be difficult to stop as this type of joint cannot be caulked.

What are the types of diagonal planking?

There are several types of diagonal planking. The first, known as double diagonal is where the planks of the inner skin start at the keel rebate and run diagonally to the deck line. The planks of the outer skin are laid similarly from the keel rebate to deck line but in the opposite direction, so that they cross each other at approximately 90° (*Fig. 3a*).

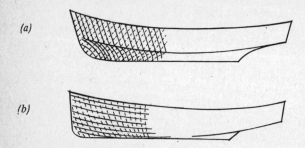

(a)

(b)

Fig. 3(a) The double diagonal chine hull. (b) A
'single' diagonal round bilge hull

There is a membrane of oiled calico or other material between the layers of planking. It is usual for the fastenings, of which there are a great number, to be copper nails with roves and clenched.

This type of construction is very strong and fewer frames are necessary than with most types of planking. It has the disadvantage that, in the event of rot or damage to the inner skin, repair is difficult and costly.

There is also a type of planking known as single diagonal (*Fig. 3b*). With this type the inner skin is laid from keel rebate to the deck line, and the outer skin laid fore and aft with close butted seams. This type does not suffer from the curling or lifting of the plank edges often found with double diagonal.

Describe the strip planking method

If strip planking is executed with care it will result in a very strong hull. The simplicity of construction is much favoured by the amateur boatbuilder for boats and, also, yachts of considerable size.

The planking is narrow, often nearly square in section, each plank being close fitted to the next, glued, and fastened through its plane. The ends of the planks are run random and are planed or sawn off at the deck line (*Fig. 4a*). When built the whole structure becomes a homogeneous mass having no seams and needing few frames.

(a)

(b)

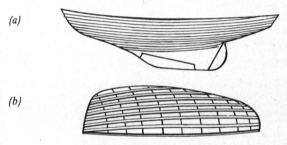

Fig. 4(a) A strip planked yacht. (b) A batten mould for moulded construction

Because of the expansion and contraction characteristics of various timbers this type of craft should be built of a stable hardwood such as iroko or teak. Repairs are rather difficult and the satisfactory glueing of the planking is of the utmost importance.

What is moulded construction?

This is a very strong construction much used for dinghies and motor boat hulls as well as for large class ocean racing boats. The hull is constructed over a mould, usually of batten construction (*Fig. 4b*).

The planking consists of several layers of thin veneers glued together so as to form a type of plywood. It is possible to build a very accurate and fair hull and, because of this, many mould hulls for the fibreglass boat industry are often built by this method.

What special precautions should be taken when using plywood?

Plywood is a deservedly popular material for amateur construction.

Fig. 4(c) A multi chine plywood hull

Usually boats built of plywood are of chine or multi-chine form (*Fig. 4c*). If considering building in ply, it is important to remember the following points:

(a) That the plan or design has no compound curves as the capability of ply to bend in this way is strictly limited.

(b) That the ply conforms to BS 1088 or 4097 as appropriate.

(c) That the glue used to scarf sheets together should be to BS 1204.

2

SETTING UP

What drawings or plans are necessary?

(a) *The construction plan.* This will give the details of the plan, sections and profile, also relevant structural details.

(b) *Lines plan.* A general plan giving the waterlines, buttocks, diagonals and sheerline, etc, also a plan showing the shape at each station with diagonals. All measurements are usually given on this plan to enable the vessel to be 'laid off' full size (*Fig. 5*).

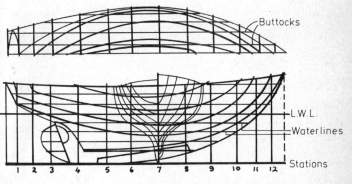

Fig. 5. A lines plan

(c) *The table of offsets.* This is a table drawn up by the designer so that the plans can be laid off without inaccurate scaling of the lines plan.

(d) *The sail and*   enable these parts to be made.

(e) *The specifica*   a complete schedule of all the materials, etc, to be   . the construction of the boat.

(f) *The rigging plan.*

What is meant by lofting?

This is the process of transferring the plans or blueprints into full-size intepretation on a floor or series of boards. These boards are usually painted matt black to provide a good contrast with the chalked lines.

With small craft it is quite possible to use sheets of hardboard or similar material and marking with a pencil or pen.

Laying out the plans to full size enables accurate patterns and templates to be made; it also shows up any discrepancy in lines, thus enabling the loftsman to fair these off.

What is the purpose of a table of offsets?

The table of offsets will be drawn up by the designer and should be attached to the plans.

The offsets relate particularly to the body plan. A table of offsets would appear similar to (*Fig. 6*).

Half breadths

Station	1	2	3	4	5	6	7
Deck	0-10-2	1-6-0	2-3-3	3-0-5	3-7-4	3-10-4	
+3							
+2							
+1			E.T.C.				
L.W.L.							
-1							
-2							
C.L.							
A							
B							
C							
D							
Sheer							

Fig. 6. A table of offsets

8

The measurements on the table are normally expressed in feet, inches and sixteenths, e.g. half breadth at LWL on station 6, 8 ft 6¼ in would appear as 8 – 6 – 4. The decimal system is also used and here the measurements are expressed entirely in millimetres.

The offsets enable the body plan to be laid out full size.

Any attempt to scale the body plan from the drawings would result in inaccuracies due to the unstable nature of paper in different atmospheric conditions. Even the thickness of a pen line when scaled up may be subject to great variation.

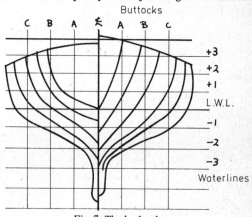

Fig. 7. The body plan

How are the offsets transferred to the mould loft floor?

(a) First draw or scribe in the centreline or vertical.

(b) Square off this line and draw in waterline LWL.

(c) Square off the centreline and draw in other waterlines as shown on table.

(d) Measure off from centreline and draw in the buttock lines.

(e) Check to ascertain that all lines are true and accurate.

The grid that has been constructed will enable (by measuring off the waterlines, centreline and buttocks) an accurate body plan to be drawn (*Fig. 7*).

Any inaccuracies should show up during this process and can then be faired off.

How are the plan curves drawn on the 'floor'?

Transfer the measurements from the table of offsets, etc. to the floor. A series of weights or a line of nails driven and left proud along the marks will help to curve a batten to be bent to a fair curve and the line drawn in (*Fig. 8a*).

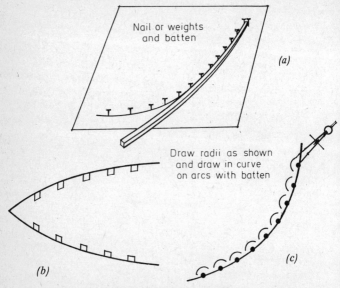

Fig. 8. Planking thickness and bevel. (a) Marking curve of frame etc. (b) Bevel on frames. (c) Marking off thickness of plank

How is the plank thickness taken off?

The plan on the floor is full size, i.e. drawn to the outside of the planking. Therefore the thickness of the plank must be taken off to obtain the correct size and bevel to enable the moulds, frames, patterns or bulkheads to be made up.

There are various methods of doing this and it must be remembered that there will be a bevel at all the stations except maybe at amidships (*Fig. 8b*).

The simplest method of taking off the plank is by drawing a series of arcs with the compasses (*Fig. 8c*).

Finding the bevel or angle at the various stations is best achieved by making up a bevel board.

How is a shape lifted from the loft floor?

On a large job this is done by measurements, marking in and drawing direct.

With smaller jobs, however, one of several methods can be used. The tack method is effective, simple, and has good results: carefully lay a line of tacks horizontally so that the heads follow the drawn line.

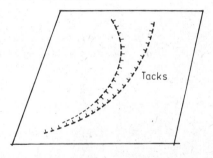

Fig. 9. The tack transfer method

Carefully place the timber of the mould, pattern or part on the tacks, and press down. When the part is removed it will show the imprint of the line of tack heads so that the line can be drawn in (*Fig. 9*).

Other methods use tracing or carbon paper.

How are moulds or patterns made?

These can be of ply for small craft such as canoes, etc but ply is a difficult material to bevel and is also costly. The best method is the traditional one whereby the moulds are built up of soft-wood; deal is satisfactory (*Fig. 10*).

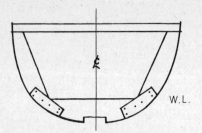

Fig. 10. A built up station mould

It is sometimes possible to make the actual bulkheads to be fitted and act as permanent moulds as would be the case with a composite or steel vessel.

What comprises the backbone of the boat?

The backbone consists of the stem, apron, stem knee, keel, hog, deadwoods, sternpost and/or transom. These parts are shaped and sided before jointing together.

How are these parts jointed together?

The keel and hog are either glued or bedded together and can be fastened with screws, clenched rods or bolted with nuts and bolts.

If the keel or hog are long and have a joint, this should be in the form of a scarf, preferably of the hooked type and in a keel joint there should be a stopwater fitted in the line of the rebate which will be covered by the planking. This stopwater is often omitted if the joint is glued (*Fig. 11*).

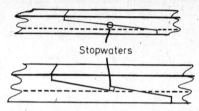

Fig. 11. Lipped scarfs with stopwaters

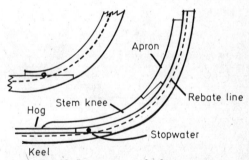

Fig. 12. Stem, apron to keel arrangements

The stem having been carefully shaped will now be scarfed to the keel. There are several methods of doing this (*Fig. 12*).

The stem knee is now fitted having first been sided. If there is to be an apron, a scarf is cut at its upper end.

The stem knee is fastened right through the stem, keel and hog scarf with bolts or clenched rods arranged as shown on the plans or as demanded by the specifications (*Fig. 13*).

13

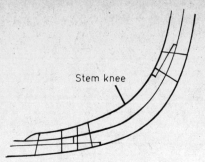

Fig. 13. Stem fastening layout

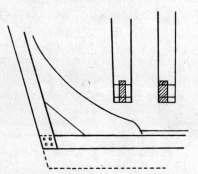

Fig. 14. Stern post keel joints

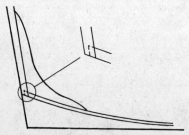

Fig. 15. Transom and stern knee

14

If the vessel is canoe or cruiser sterned, the fitting method would be the same as at the stem.

Deadwoods are fitted on the top of the keel in good construction. If the boat is to have a stern post it must be scarfed or half-jointed to the aft end of the keel (*Fig. 14*).

A transom stern is jointed to the keel. This joint may run right through, but it will be a neater and better job checked halfway through (*Fig. 15*).

If the craft has an iron or lead keel, when would this be fitted?

It is usual to build the wood keel and the structure of the boat direct onto the metal keel resting on its blocks.

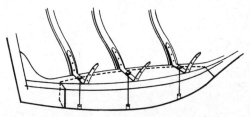

Fig. 16. Arrangement of ballast keel fixing

The metal keel, if made of lead, may be cast *in situ*, or in the case of an iron keel, cast at the foundry and then set up afterwards (*Fig. 16*).

How are the keel bolts fitted with a metal keel?

(a) In a lead keel the holes may be drilled through after the casting has been done, or formed by inserting rods into the mould before casting takes place.

(b) In an iron keel the holes will be drilled or may be cast in at the foundry.

The bolts must be of a material compatible with the metal of the keel, e.g. bronze with lead (galvanised iron is sometimes

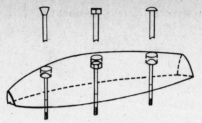

Fig. 17. Keel counterbores and types of bolts

used), and steel with iron. Lloyds recommendations should be followed for bolt sizes.

The heads of the bolts or nuts must be sunk into a counterbore in the bottom of the keel and the hole stopped with a suitable compound which is waterproof. This stopping must be removable in case of renewal of bolts, etc (*Fig. 17*).

How is the keel set up?

It is usual to set the keel up on blocks of a suitable building height so that the declivity is correct, i.e. so that the bulkheads would be upright and the waterline level, in the position the boat is intended to assume when afloat (*Fig. 18*).

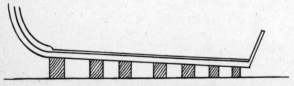

Fig. 18. Setting up a keel, or backbone

The top of the stem and stern post or transom and maybe the moulds, if necessary, are braced by temporary fixings to a building or other convenient place. The whole backbone structure is carefully checked for being upright with level and plumbline.

How are the moulds and bulkheads set up?

The actual number of moulds will depend on the shape and type of vessel. If the vessel is to have a number of bulkheads, these can be erected in their finished condition to advantage.

The moulds or bulkheads are fitted to the hog. Moulds are usually fixed by a small removable block screwed to the hog (*Fig. 19*).

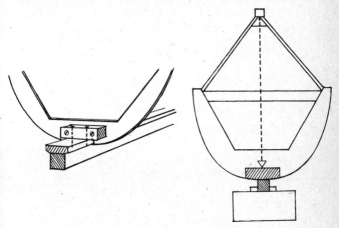

Fig. 19. Setting up the moulds

Check each mould carefully for being upright and true. This can be done with a plumbline from the centreline or with a spirit level. Fix the moulds and re-check for true.

If the boat is to have a centreline engine installation how is the position for the stern tube found and the pilot hole bored?

The shaft line should be shown on the drawings of the boat.

Erect a bracket, or if possible use a mould or bulkhead at the forward end of the engine space. Work off the shaft height at this point. Square this off and transfer this mark outboard to clear the keel.

Fix a temporary bracket at the outside end, this can be fixed to the transom. Mark off the height of the shaft line, transfer this mark by squaring off to clear the keel. Run a chalk line, or wire, between the marks and fix. The line of the wire can then be transferred to the keel and marked in (*Fig. 20*).

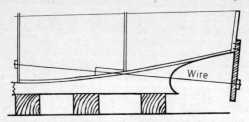

Fig. 20. Marking off the stern tube

This will enable a drill or boring bar to be rigged (see Chapter 7 for boring out details).

3

CARVEL PLANKING

What are the methods used in carvel planking a boat?

In very small craft, where, for instance, the planking runs the full length of the hull, it is possible to mark off and spile planking in the same way as the normal method of clencher building (see Chapter 4).

If, however, it is a large boat it is more usual to steam bend the timbers into place before planking commences. In the case of sawn or grown frames, these are erected fully bevelled and faired.

How are the timbers steamed and fitted?

(a) The backbone and moulds are erected as described in Chapter 2.

(b) The hull is then 'battened up'. A number of battens, which must be in excess of the length of the boat, are temporarily fastened to the stem and transom and run fair and true over the moulds. The number of battens used will depend on the curvature of the surface at that section, i.e. more battens are needed at the turn of bilge and the reverse tuck towards aft, than on the flat topside sections.

(c) The timbers are then steamed and bent into position. Only experience will determine the length of steaming time necessary for various sizes of timber.

The main requirement of the steaming box will be length in order to take the longest timber. The steam must be saturated otherwise the timber will become dry and brittle.

When shored and wedged into position against the battens the timbers should be fastened to the hog or top of the keel.

How is carvel planking laid out?

Careful thought must be given to the planking width on a boat with a sharp turn of bilge. The planks will necessarily be narrower at this point than on the much flatter section of the topsides or further down towards the garboard.

Very careful allowance must be made for plank thickness as it is necessary to plane the planks to any curvature on the inside face and when fastened to be planed smooth on the outside. Therefore the planking will be of greater thickness at the turn of bilge and any tuck the vessel may have towards aft.

Arrangement of plank butts with
alternate sawn and bent frames

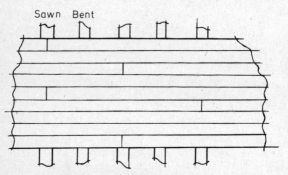

Fig. 21. Arrangement of butts

Unless it is a small vessel it will not be possible to obtain or fit planks in one continuous length and in these circumstances it will be necessary to make a plan of the layout of butts or plank ends. Lloyds rules set out recommendations for this. These are, generally speaking, that no plank butt must be within 4 ft of another, also that no two butts are on the same frame or timber within three spaces of another, or if using butt straps within three vertical spaces (*Fig. 21*).

How are the planks marked off?

The division of planking is best done by marking off at the stem at a regular width and then running a long batten from those marks over the moulds and marking when satisfied with the curve produced. This trial and error method produces the best results and is well worth the time spent sighting through and adjusting. Care should be taken to make an attractive layout if the boat is to be varnished.

How is carvel 'taken off'?

(a) This is done by spiling, and several spiling battens of varying widths will be required. These battens must be in excess of the boat's length which can be done by joining several pieces together, or by cramping together, i.e. wider battens are necessary where the shape is greatest. The battens must be thin and pliable enough to be curved around the length of the hull fairly and true.

(b) The spiling batten is cramped or wedged in position starting with the garboard. The marks are then carefully transferred or scribed on the spiling batten. The batten is then taken off and the resultant marking transferred to the plank so that it may be cut and shaped prior to fitting.

In which order is the planking fitted?

The garboard is usually fitted first, then the planking continued upwards to the sheerstrake. Some boatbuilders start at random in order to use the planks for wedging down neighbouring planks (*Fig. 22a*).

How is the garboard strake fitted?

Having been cut to approximate size from the spiling batten, the plank is now offered up and cramped into as close a position as possible. The plank can then be marked for final fitting, making sure that it is a perfect fit throughout its length, particular attention being paid to the fit into the forefoot rebate on the stem. When satisfied that the plank is ready for fitting the caulking allowance can be planed on (*Fig. 22b*).

It is a good practice to prime the rebate and the plank edges, etc, before finally cramping into position. It is a help to fix temporary cleats to the timbers near the plank so that wedges can be used to harden the plank into place. (*Fig. 22c*).

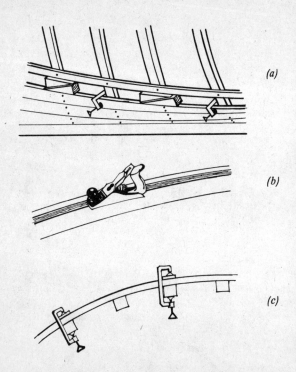

(a)

(b)

(c)

Fig. 22. Planking methods. (a) Plank cramping up. (b) Planing on caulking allowance. (c) Wedging and cramping planking

How is the plank fastened off?

The number of fastenings depends entirely on the width of plank (see Lloyds rules). The plank is marked off then drilled and counterbored to take the head of the fastening, the pilot hole in the frame will depend on whether the planking is being screw or clench fastened.

How are the rest of the planks fitted?

Use the same method as with the garboard, working up the hull to the sheerstrake, fastening each plank as it is fitted.

If the boat has an involved shape at the ends it may entail steaming the planks into position.

Should both sides be planked up together?

If the boat has been set up correctly and care is taken it should be possible to cut both side planks off the same spiling, leaving a little excess on the timber for final fitting. Considerable time can be saved in this way.

What are the types of fastening suitable for carvel construction?

Treenails or trunnels; screws; nails or dumps; copper nails and roves clenched.

What are treenails (trunnels)?

These are wooden pegs similar to dowels. The plank and frame are drilled so that the treenails are driven in as a tight fit. In the best construction the treenails are cut and wedged both inside and out (*Fig. 23a*).

What types of screws and nails should be used?

Screw. These may be made of a number of materials and the specification will call for the particular metal required, e.g.

23

silicon bronze, monel, glavanised iron, etc. These must be drilled with the appropriate size drills for the screw shank and thread, and then counterbored into the planking so that the head of the fastening can be stopped or dowels glued in and then planed off.

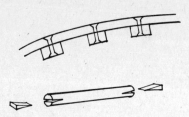

Fig. 23. Fastenings for carvel. (a) The treenail or trunnel

Nails or dumps. For the best results these should be of the cut type. Nowadays these are usually galvanised but can be dipped into hot Swedish or Stockholm tar if for a workboat. The planking must be drilled and counterbored, with a pilot hole drilled into the frame or stem, etc. When driven, the fastening is sunk into the counterbore so that the head can be covered with stopping etc. These nails are found in older fishing boats and are satisfactory in low price construction.

Describe the copper nail and roves clenched method of construction

This is by far the most popular method of fastening in wooden yacht construction, probably for the very good reason that it is the strongest type of fastening if carried out properly.

The plank and frame are drilled to the appropriate size, then the plank is counterbored. The nails are then driven and punched home to the bottom of the counterbore (*Fig. 23b*).

The head of the nail must be held with a 'dolly' whilst the rove is punched on with a special rove punch, the nail is then

24

clipped off close to the rove. A little experience will soon determine just how much to leave showing through. Then, whilst being held securely on the head with the dolly, the nail is rivetted over the rove.

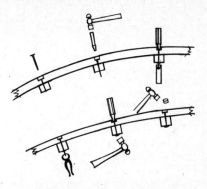

Fig. 23. Fastenings for carvel. (b) Clenching for carvel planking

This is a powerful method of drawing the planking home. The counterbore is stopped or dowelled.

4

CLENCHER PLANKING

What are the special tools and items needed for planking a clencher hull?

(a) A number of spiling battens, i.e. wide pieces of thin wood, usually thinner than the planking and in excess of the boat's length and capable of being bent around the shape of the hull at all the waterlines.

(b) Sighting battens, long fair flexible battens for marking off and setting out the planking etc.

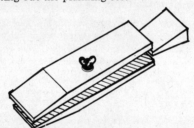

Fig. 24. Clencher planking wedge cramp or nipper

(c) Wooden wedge cramps and wedges (*Fig. 24*).

(d) Rove punch, nail cutters and dolly for holding on to nail heads.

Which way up is a clencher boat built?

The boat can be built either way up to the preference of the builder. The stocks can be set up as shown in *Fig. 25*.

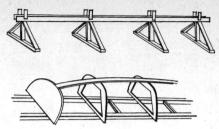

Fig. 25. Dinghy stocks

How are the moulds made up?

These are built up with pieces of softwood, joined together (*Fig. 26a*). Deal is a good material for this purpose. The moulds are to be set up on the keel at the number of stations required.

How are the moulds set up?

They can be held on the keel with a small block or blocks screwed on each side and screwed down (*Fig. 26b*). The upper

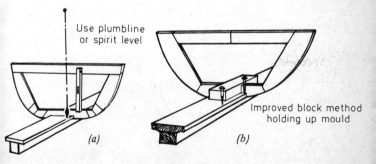

Use plumbline or spirit level

(a)

Improved block method holding up mould

(b)

Fig. 26. Setting up moulds. (a) Lining up mould. (b) Improved holding block

side is held up by braces from any convenient part of the building and then squared up with the keel and plumbed to upright with the centreline. The moulds should have the correct bevel planed on before fitting.

By which method is the planking set out?

It is usual for the boatbuilder to set out the planking by eye, using a true flexible batten by marking along the moulds in a fair curve. The planks will be about the same width at the stem, but will vary from the garboard strake from fairly wide depending on the shape at the ends of the boat, to narrower on the turn of bilge and widening again on the flatter section of the topsides to the sheerstrake.

This narrowing of the turn of bilge planking is necessary to prevent distortion of the planks on the sharper curve of the midship section (*Fig. 27a*).

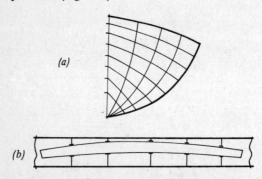

(a)

(b)

Fig. 27. Marking out clencher planking. (a) Marking off hull moulds. (b) The spiling batten

It is necessary to spend a good deal of time and trouble offering up the batten and sighting through before an acceptable curve is found.

The sheer and the whole of the planking must be perfectly proportioned for a clencher boat to look good.

28

In which order is the planking fitted and how is this done?

The garboard is fitted first. This is usually a fairly wide board and should be left in excess of the finished width until the rebate and keel fitting edge have been worked to a satisfactory fit.

The plank is first offered up and cramped into position close to the keel and rebates. It is then spiled off, marked out, and cut.

It is good policy to leave the size slightly proud so that the rebate end can be fitted accurately. It may take several tries before a perfect fit is achieved.

When the plank is ready for fitting its upper edge can be cut to the marked out width. It should be possible to cut the plank for the other side if the keel and moulds have been set up accurately.

The plank should be then bedded on, holding it firmly in place with the wedge clamps. The garboard should then be fastened off at the stem, along the hog and at the transom.

When this has been done the other planks can be spiled off, one at a time, with the spiling batten which is cramped up into place and scribed or marked off carefully. The slope is then carefully transferred to the planking (*Fig. 27b*).

If the planking cannot be fitted full length, how is it scarfed together?

Scarfs should be as long as possible, and with this in mind, the plain scarf has such fine feather ends as to be impractical for good fitting. It is preferable to make a lipped scarf (*Fig. 28a*).

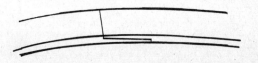

Fig. 28. Scarf for clencher planking. (a) A lipped scarf

This joint must either be bedded or glued together. Resorcinol glue makes an excellent joint which does not need fastening — a great advantage as fastenings tend to split the timber. When gluing up it is necessary to coat both surfaces and to cramp together with pads to ensure that the faces of

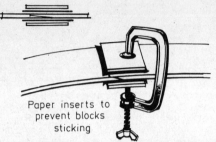

Fig. 28. Scarf for clencher planking. (b) Gluing
a plank scarf

the scarf do not warp (*Fig. 28b*). Paper should be inserted between the pads and the plank face to prevent sticking of the cramping pads.

How are the plank edges of lands fitted?

As each plank is offered up it must be marked and cut with a suitable bevel or rebate which is accentuated towards the plank ends. This must be in complete contact with the stem or transom (*Fig. 29a*).

A bevel is better than a rebate at the stem but involves a fair amount of practice to attain a perfect job. Each plank about the turn of bilge will have some form of bevel to take its neighbour.

The planks are fastened as they are fitted. It is necessary to drill for the fastenings to prevent the timber from splitting.

The fastenings will be between the stations or frame positions, frames or timbers are fitted at a later stage. Each plank and its mating surface should be well painted or varnished before final fastening.

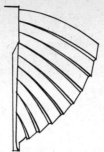

*Fig. 29. Planking ar-
rangements. (a) Planking
at stem*

The garboard can be fastened with nails but screws make a
stronger job.

Great care should be used when nailing the plank 'hood
ends' so that they do not split. The sheerstrake is often of a
contrasting timber, to give an attractive appearance when
varnished.

FRAMING AND TIMBERING

What sort of framing is used in clencher boats?

In small boats, steamed or bent timbers are almost universal,
whereas, in larger boats they may be alternatively sawn and
steamed. Young oak, rock elm, acacia or American white
oak are the best materials for this purpose. Ash can be used
but is not durable.

Timbers can be bent dry, steamed, or soaked in fresh water
for a few days.

What method is used for fitting framing?

The first step is to select good straight grained material free from
knots or faults. It should then be prepared, cut and planed to
size. The inward edges should be slightly relieved to take off
the sharp corners.

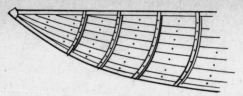

Fig. 29. Planking arrangements. (b) Fastening layout

Frames or timbers should, if possible, be full length. When the material has been steamed or soaked (if necessary), it can be pushed gently down into position holding down with lengths of wood as shores with a pad at the point of contact to spread the load and so prevent a crack or fracture occurring at the bend. A length of timber cramped across the top of the hull will provide a good shoring down point.

The timbers should be fastened off as soon as possible, preferably as soon as they are fitted. Both the planking and the timber must be drilled to take the fastening (*Fig. 29b*).

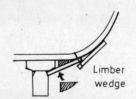

Limber wedge

Fig. 29. Planking arrangements. (c) Limber wedges

It is usually necessary to fit small wedges along the garboard strakes where the timber leaves the plank to cross the hog. A small hole should be left to provide a limber for bilge water (*Fig. 29c*).

If care is taken to bevel the hog to a good shape so that the garboard strakes lie at the correct angle, the space left between the timbers and garboards may be small enough to dispense with the wedges.

How are the gunwales fitted?

These can either be fitted inside the timbers and through
fastened, or the tops of the timbers cut down the depth of
the wood and the gunwales fitted tight to the sheerstrake
(*Fig. 30a*).

The forward ends are joggled around the corner of the
apron or stem (*Fig. 30b*). At the aft end they run square to the
transom.

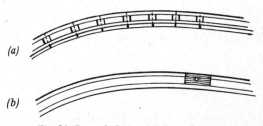

(a)

(b)

Fig. 30. Gunwale fitting. (a) Gunwale inside timbers.
(b) Gunwale above timbers

In the case of a larger, decked boat the gunwales would in
fact be the beamshelf, or clamp. This is the longitudinal member
usually fitted inside the frames at under-deck level to carry the
ends of the deck beams.

How are the forward ends of the gunwales and hull tied together?

A breast hook should be fitted. On small craft this is usually
made of wood, e.g. a grown oak crook or a laminated member.
A steel or iron fitting is sometimes used (*Fig. 31*). This member
should be through fastened.

What method is used to tie the aft ends or corners together?

Carefully selected crooks made into knees or laminated
members are used closely fitted and through fastened.

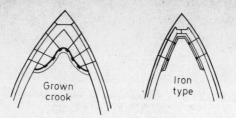

Fig. 31. Breast hooks

How are copper clenches fastened in clencher boats?

The hole for the nail should be drilled through the planking and timber and then lightly countersunk on the outside. This countersink needs to be deeper on hardwood planking where the nails do not pull into the wood as with softwoods.

When driving the nails a heavy hammer or dolly must be held on the frame close to the hole, this will cause the timber to draw home snug to the planking. The head of the nail is now held on with the dolly and the rove punched home onto the nail with the rove punch. Cut the nail off about $\frac{1}{64}$ in from the rove. This allowance will vary with the size of fastening and the type of timber used to build the hull. Only experience will provide the correct result.

The nail is now rivetted over the rove holding firmly on the head of the nail with the dolly, until the planking and frame are drawn tightly together. The rove should *not* be flattened.

5

DOUBLE SKIN CONSTRUCTION

What is the setting up method for double skin construction?

A large number of moulds are necessary for this type of
construction if it is of round bilge form – even better is a
battened mould. Double diagonal is much more often used for
chine construction and it is usual with this method to make up
the frames as moulds (*Fig. 32*).

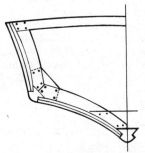

Fig. 32. Frame mould for
diagonal hull

It is necessary to fit the beamshelf and chines, etc before
planking up as these are all part of the mould.

The planking is usually fairly thin and wide.

How is the planking fitted?

Planking can start at the stem and it is normal to fit the inner
planking with the plank edges running diagonally upwards

towards aft. The planks are cut to fit the rebate and are then bent into position, cramping up wherever necessary. The rebate and the rebate ends of the planking should be primed with paint and bedded, then temporarily fastened, at the stem and at the beamshelf. Top ends of planks are usually allowed to run at random above the gunwale or sheer until the planking is completed. The whole side should be planked up, carefully wedging the planks together to a perfect fit. When the first layer of planking is complete, it should be painted completely with primer.

A membrane of calico is then stapled to the planking and soaked with linseed oil. This can be done in sections as the outer planking is fitted.

What is the method of planking the outer skin and what are the preparations?

The planking should be primed with paint on the face which will be innermost.

This inside planking runs approximately opposite to the inner layer. The first piece to be fitted is often at the forefoot of the stem as shown in *Fig. 33a*.

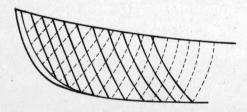

Fig. 33. Diagonal planking. (a) Arrangement of planking

It is advantageous to fit a temporary plank or batten close to the plank that is being fitted to act as a wedging base, so that the planking can be wedged up tight before fastening.

How is the planking fastened?

On the ends of the planks where these fit to the stem rebate, known as hood ends along the keel and on the transom. It can be screwed or nailed either with copper nails or ring barbed nails. These must be countersunk so that the heads may be stopped.

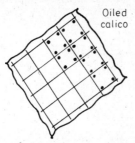

Oiled calico

Fig. 33. Diagonal planking.
(b) Square of planking

When the planking up is complete the edges of the planking on the sheerline can be cut off and the sheerline planed smooth.

Planks are fastened with copper nails and roves; the corners of each square of planking (*Fig. 33b*) are fastened, thus producing a very strong hull.

6

THE DECK

How are the deck beams fitted and which joints would be used?

The deck beams have to carry the weight of the deck and are also valuable strengthening members of the boat's structure, tying the upper part of the vessel together.

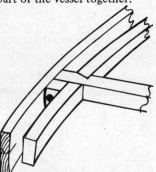

Fig. 34. Main deck beam joints

The main beam or beams in way of the mast and shroud area are usually carried right out to the planking and jointed into the beamshelf (*Fig. 34*).

What is the purpose of the carlines and how are they fitted?

The carlines are beams which lie fore and aft, their purpose is to carry the inboard ends of the beams in way of a coachroof, hatch, or skylight, etc.

These are jointed into beams as *Fig. 35(a)*.

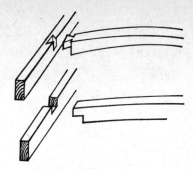

Fig. 35(a). Joints for deck beams and carlines

What are tie bars and how are they fitted?

A tie bar is a metal rod or bar fitted athwartships alongside or between the deck beams, fastened through the shelf or clamp and occasionally the frame and/or planking as well at its outer end and through a carline at the inner end.

The purpose of these bars is to obviate any movement outward of the beam end joints. These bars are usually threaded and fitted with nuts and washers (*Fig. 35b*).

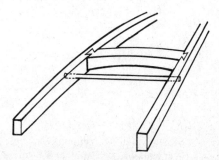

Fig. 35(b). Tie bar between carline and beamshelf

What is a 'laid' deck?

A laid deck may consist of a single layer of planking fastened directly to the beams, or may consist of a ply deck with a laid cladding (*Fig. 36*).

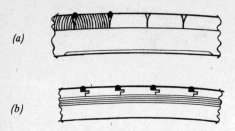

(a)

(b)

Fig. 36. (a) A traditional laid deck with V seams to take caulking cotton and marine glue or rubber compound. (b) A plywood deck with laid cladding – in this case tongue and groove.

Both types may be either caulked or splined. The planking may be laid or fitted straight fore and aft or to the covering board and a king plank.

Is there a specific way that timber should be cut for deck planking?

The timber should always be cut if possible with the grain vertical, or rift sawn. This will provide an even wearing surface that will not splinter.

Deck planking should be kept fairly narrow as the planks have to be curved outwards to the covering boards. This would be impossible to achieve with wide boards.

Wide boards also have a tendency to warp or curl up at the edges and in so doing pull the fastenings.

40

What preparation of the planking is necessary before fitting?

The planking should be planed to size on all surfaces. Also, because it is virtually impossible to lay the planks so that the underside edges are all neat and smooth, these should be bevelled or beaded on the lower edge.

This gives an attractive appearance and should be done unless the deckhead is to be lined or panelled (*Fig. 37*).

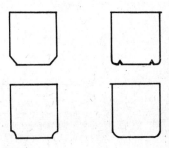

Fig. 37. Bevels and beads for beams

Next, the caulking allowance has to be considered. If the deck is to be caulked and payed in the traditional way, the top edge has to be planed to a deep narrow bevel. The depth of this bevel should be sufficient to take the cotton or oakum leaving a seam after hardening down with a depth of twice the width at the top, this will ensure a good surface for the stopping to adhere to.

If the deck is to be caulked with a rubber or synthetic stopper, the practice of using cotton or oakum is not recommended and the seam should be made square or rectangular.

41

It is good practice to make the seams wide enough, remembering that rubber will only expand or contract as far as its bulk will allow. Thus, on a deck with planks 2 in wide a seam of ¼ in width would be adequate.

If in doubt the manufacturer's literature should be consulted.

What is the king plank and how is it fitted?

The king plank is the centre board in a deck which is to be laid with the planking curved to the shape of the boat. It can have straight plain edges or it may be joggled so that each plank end fits into the notch or joggle. This joggle looks like a flat scarf (*Fig. 38a*).

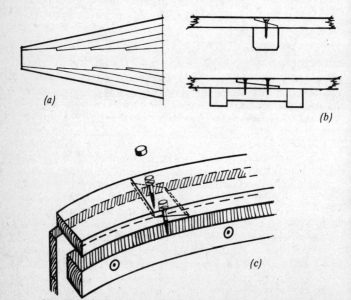

(a)

(b)

(c)

Fig. 38. King plank and covering board detail. (a) King plank edges. (b) King plank scarf or butt. (c) Covering board scarf

The king plank should be fitted from the stem to run aft as far as possible (to the coachroof or skylight, etc) and then continuing after of the cockpit to stern post or transom. If it is necessary to scarf this plank this should preferably be a glued scarf in way of a deck beam or alternatively a butt strap (*Fig. 38b*). As the king plank may be a considerable width compared with the deck planking, it is usually screwed down. The holes for the fastenings should be counterbored for dowels to be glued in to cover the heads of the fastenings.

The fore and aft end joints should be a tight fit with a caulking allowance.

If the planking is to be laid to the curve of the covering board and fitted to a king plank, the width of the planking may be graduated throughout its length to look more attractive when finished.

What are the covering boards and how are they fitted?

The covering boards are the planks or boards at each side of the deck planking. These boards cover the top of the outer planking (sheerstrake) and frames or timbers. It is normal for the covering boards to be made the same thickness as the decking, and about three times the planking width.

With careful selection of material it is possible to get the grain of the timber to follow the line or curve of the hull.

Any joints between lengths should be scarfed and glued (see *Fig. 38c*). If this is not possible boards must be joined with a part butt strap to take the part not supported by the beamshelf or hull planking.

Sometimes the outer edge of the board, if not to be covered by a moulding or rubbing strake or band, is run over slightly with a rounded edge for improved appearance (*Fig. 39a*).

The board should be thoroughly bedded onto the top edge of the outer plank and well fastened to prevent the ingress of water. At the fore end, the board must be cut to fit around the stem and should be fastened through its plane.

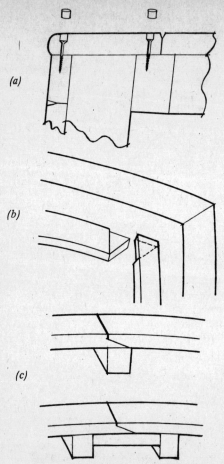

Fig. 39. Covering board and deck plank
detail. (a) Covering board edge. (b) Joint
for aft end covering board. (c) Deck
planking scarf

The board is usually screwed down and there should be fastenings into each deck beam as well as into the beam shelf and outer planking.

At the aft end the covering boards are jointed to the athwartships board across the counter or transom (*Fig. 39b*).

What is the procedure for laying the deck?

Unless the vessel is quite small, it is unlikely that the deck planks can be laid full length. Thus it is necessary to work out the shift of butts, this should be to the same formula as for hull planking in Chapter 3.

The butts can be fastened direct on to the beams if the deck beams are of sufficient scantling. A somewhat better job is achieved by scarfing the ends together, gluing and then through fastening either to a deck beam or a butt strap (*Fig. 39c*).

Each plank is laid on the beams and wedged out to be in hard contact with the next. It is then fastened down.

What types of deck fastening are used?

The decking may be fastened with nails, preferably of the ring barbed type.

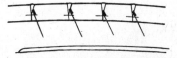

Fig. 40. (a) Secret nail detail

The nails are driven through the edge of the planking as shown in *Fig. 40a*. The planks must be drilled for these nails or the wood will almost certainly split.

Nails must be punched under flush so that they do not interfere with the caulking. This method is known as secret fastening.

Another method of fastening is with screws or ring barbed nails. The holes for these must be drilled and counterbored;

45

these holes are afterwards stopped with dowels glued into place. This type of deck fastening gives the advantage of being more easily repaired.

If the deck is of light scantling or if the beams are widely spaced, it may be necessary to fit side dowels into the plank edges.

Plank ends should be fastened laterally where they joint to the king plank.

What is the sequence for a straight laid deck?

It is normal to start off with the centre plank and fasten this off. Then, working both ways, fit and fasten each plank in its finished position. This is a straightforward job as it is a simple matter to wedge the straight planks into position.

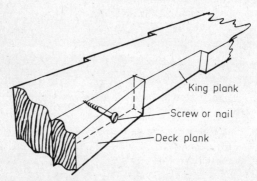

Fig. 40. (b) Lateral king plank fastening. Plank ends should be fastened laterally where they join the king plank

The edges must all be a tight fit, with a similar caulking allowance to a curved deck. The ends of the planks will run out to the covering board (*Fig. 40b*) and must be fixed to the beamshelf.

If the top edge of the beamshelf is not level with deck beams there is no satisfactory method of fastening the deck

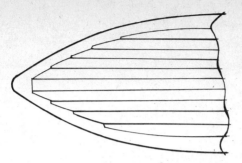

*Fig. 40. (c) Straight plank deck to covering board,
scarf style*

plank ends to the covering board. In this case the planking is
laid from the covering board inwards, each plank being fastened
off laterally in a similar fashion as plank fastenings to a king
plank.

A normal allowance for caulking is made at each plank end
and along the joint with the covering board.

This type of deck can be secret fastened or screwed and
dowelled.

It does not look as attractive as a curved, planked deck but
is more economical on both labour and materials.

What is a sheathed plywood deck and what are its advantages?

This is a plywood deck of total coverage which is covered with
a skin of more durable or more decorative planking. Properly
executed this should be completely leakproof and both very
strong and lighter than an ordinary laid deck.

What are the methods used for laying sheathed plywood decking?

The plywood should be laid in as large sections as possible and
the joints kept to beams or carlines and screwed or nailed down,
or fitted with screwed butt straps. As the deck is to be covered
with another layer of timber it is usually considered unnecessary
to scarf the joints of the plywood.

In superior work the plywood is fitted out to and fastened onto the beamshelf (where possible) and the covering board made the same total thickness as that of the deck and plywood together, the inner edge of the covering board being rebated so that the outer seam of the top layer of planking abutts the covering board. (*Fig. 41a*).

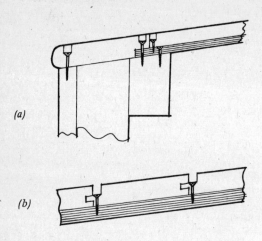

Fig. 41. *Covering board and planking detail for wood sheathed deck. (a) Detail of covering board, beam shelf etc. (b) Secret fastening*

The plywood can also be laid so that the ply runs to the outside of the plank edge and a false covering board fitted. With this method it is very important to seal the edge of the plywood with a waterproof resin to prevent the ingress of moisture to the cores.

The best material for the outer skin of planking is teak, with iroko a reasonable substitute. Each plank should be laid in a liberal coating of glue (*Fig. 41b*). Softwoods are unsuitable because of their greater water absorption which causes excess movement at the seams and possible glue line failure.

Softwood decking is best secret fastened with screws or ring barbed nails.

What are the advantages of a glass fibre sheathed ply deck and how is this undertaken?

On light craft this type of deck offers a popular alternative to canvas covered decking. If carried out properly it makes a light strong deck which is completely waterproof.

When laying the plywood deck, care is needed in making sure that the scarfs and butts are sound and that there is no possibility of movement, as this would soon crack the surface of the glass fibre layer.

The plywood must be perfectly clean and dry. Any stoppings and fillers that are used over fastenings, etc must be compatible with the covering resin, e.g. polyester or epoxy.

The workshop temperature should be controlled if possible to 60°F (15°C) or above whilst carrying out the job and until the curing is complete.

The type of matt or cloth used is largely a matter of preference, and the weight of the material will depend on the likely usage of the deck. For example a workboat's deck which will be used roughly will need a heavy covering, but for a small boat where the covering only serves to waterproof the deck, a light cloth or roving will be all that is necessary.

How are plastic deck coverings applied?

A deck of plywood is not capable of withstanding heavy traffic or abrasion without damage to the surface veneers.

Covering the deck with a good quality plastic decking can solve this problem, and may also make the deck largely non-slip.

As with any covering the deck must be clean and dry and any fillings or stopper used must be compatible with the adhesive used to glue the plastic down. If in doubt seek the manufacturers' advice.

Most adhesives used for this application are petroleum based, calling for stringent safety precautions because of the inflammable vapour. This vapour may also be harmful to the operators.

Generally speaking the best method of application of the material is to cut the pieces roughly to size, remembering that thermoplastics are inclined to shrink. If possible, the pieces should be rolled and the adhesive applied to a moderate area at a time; the material is then rolled into place. Take care to ensure that no stray pieces of hard substance get onto the adhesive and also that no air bubbles are trapped.

If the best quality plastic covering is used, there will be no need to batten or cover the joins in the material.

How is a deck prepared for laying canvas?

The plywood or planking must be clean, and all fastenings and uneven areas made up, preferably with a modern synthetic stopper. Seams must also be stopped in a similar manner.

The whole deck must be scraped and planed smooth then sanded down.

In the case of an older boat where the seams have become wider or there is movement, the deck must be stripped of any tarry or bituminous substances, any looseness of caulking made good and any movement between planks or members stopped.

If a soft stopper is used, the canvas covering will show unsightly lumps at the seams during prolonged wet weather as the mass of the deck increases its moisture content.

It is better to (a) spline the seams with wooden splines glued in, or (b) stop with a hard synthetic stopper, or (c) cover the whole deck with thin plywood well glued or bedded down and fastened with screws or ring barbed nails.

All deck fittings and mouldings must be removed to make a satisfactory job.

The deck should then be sanded and primed with a good primer.

There are several methods of applying the canvas, each way having its advocates among boatbuilders.

Adhesive compound such as Jefferies No. 3, or a good oil-based paint, can be used to bed the canvas in. Synthetic paints are, generally speaking, too hard and lack flexibility.

The canvas should be of a grade or weight to suit the particular job, e.g. 10 or 12 oz cloth on the deck of a yacht which will get hard wear whilst sail handling etc. down to a heavy grade calico on the coachroof of a motor cruiser which has only occasional traffic. As the whole object of the canvas is to provide a membrane for keeping the paint together, the lightest, most open weave is usually best.

The canvas may be cut roughly to shape and then rolled up. Working from forward, apply paint or glue thickly to the deck for say 3 ft. Then tack the end of the canvas down and roll gently back onto the paint, brushing down as it is laid to make certain that the paint oozes into the weave of the cloth. Carefully fit the canvas around the hatches, etc and tack each shift as it is laid.

When the canvas is laid, the whole surface should be painted and left to dry. Gloss paint should not be used, as this hardens and chips. When the deck has been painted, the mouldings and fittings can be fitted and bedded down.

7

STRUCTURAL DETAILS

MOUNTING OF MACHINERY

What are the main requirements of engine beds?

These should be of a good hardwood, e.g. teak, well seasoned oak or pitch pine. The timber should be well seasoned and stable to prevent subsequent problems with engine alignment. Mahogany is unsuitable as it suffers decay when in contact with ferrous metals. Engine beds should be as long as possible, of heavy scantling with adequate floors and gussets so that the load is spread over as much of the boat as possible. Transverse beds should be fitted carefully over their entire length close to the planking and if possible well fitted over the longitudinal stringers.

A resiliently mounted engine requires just as much holding down as a solidly mounted engine.

How is the engine bed position found for fitting?

Piano wire is the best medium, this is erected between a wood or metal bracket cramped to a convenient position on the outside of the stern, run through the stern tube hole or pilot hole to either a bracket cramped up or preferably the forward engine space bulkhead to the angle or line shown on the drawings or plans. This can be done by measuring up from the top of the hog and squaring off to the centre line. The wire must be very tight with no sag.

This is now the shaft line. It will be possible, using the engine specification to find the height and position of the engine

52

mounts or supports, and by measuring and squaring off the wire to make up the bed patterns.

The engine bed must be made slightly lower than the designed height to allow for lining up shims or packers under the engine supports (*Fig. 42*).

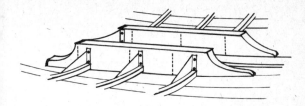

Fig. 42. Engine beds showing gussets, etc

The beds should be through fastened, preferably through the floors and planking. Fastenings can be bolts, or rods clenched over washers. The nuts should be set in oversize counterbores to allow for tightening of the nuts with a box spanner.

How is the stern tube aligned?

The hole for the stern tube must be bored out from the pilot size described in Chapter 2 to a good tight fit for the stern tube. In a very small craft this can be done by simply drilling out with an auger set up on a bracket. This method would not be accurate for a larger craft with a long tube, where it would be necessary to set up a boring bar.

How is the boring bar set up?

With the wire in position, mark off the centres at the fore and aft ends, the wire is now taken down.

Fit the boring bar bearings and brackets. It may be necessary to rig some form of temporary supports to take the bar. A boring bar can be hand operated but is usually driven by an electric motor or heavy duty drill. The r.p.m. must be slow. Great care must be taken not to cut too much at each run through, otherwise the tool may dig in and jam, or flex, making the resulting bore inaccurate.

Test the bore frequently with calipers until the finished size is achieved.

What is the method for installing the stern tube?

There are various forms of stern tube (*Fig. 43a*). The normal type has the forward and aft end bearing and glands, etc screwed on.

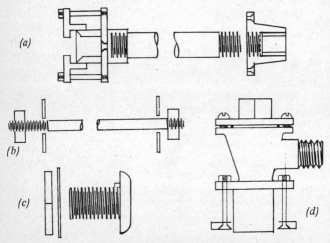

Fig. 43. Stern gear. (a) Stern tube detail. (b) Tube drawing bar. (c) Screwed type skin fitting. (d) Tapered cone flage type skin fitting

When fitting, the tube is drawn home with a draw bar (*Fig. 43b*). The tube should be liberally smeared and bedded with a waterproof compound. Traditionally this is white lead putty with a little tallow mixed in to make it work more easily.

54

When the tube has been drawn home, the fore and aft end glands and bearing can be fitted. These should be screwed up tight onto the stern tube chock or deadwood, and fastened.

How would a P or A bracket be lined up and fitted?

It will be necessary to first rig the sight wire through the stern tube, lining this up accurately and supporting it outboard and clear with a temporary bracket. An easy way is to thread the bracket onto the wire as it is rigged and support it clear of the wire. The bracket can then be lined up, using blocks, wedges, etc until accurately in line, testing with calipers at both ends of the bearing. The pads between the hull and bracket can now be measured and made up. These are put into position and the fastenings drilled off. The pads are then bedded in with compound, the bolts knocked home, well bedded with a turn of cotton around the head if necessary, and then tightened up. Re-check to make sure that the alignment is correct.

SKIN FITTINGS

How are skin fittings and valves fitted?

There are many types of fitting. They should be made of high quality bronze or similar non-corroding material.

If possible it is best to fit skin fittings so that the plank edges are not cut, and there should always be a between-frame chock or pad bedded and fastened on to the inside of the planking in way of the fitting. The purpose of this pad is both to add strength and provide a flat surface for the flange of the fitting to lie against. If there is an outside flange, this should be sunk in to be flat.

Skin fittings should be well bedded with a waterproof compound. The bolts and nuts should have washers fitted with a turn of cotton as well as the compound.

With screwed-type through-hull fittings, the hole should be a good tight fit and a pad fitted as with an ordinary flange fitting. There is usually a locating nib or block on screwed fittings to stop them turning whilst the nut is tightened. They must be liberally coated with bedding compound and a backing washer must be fitted (*Fig. 43c*).

How should an anchor winch be sited and fixed?

The primary consideration is that the winch should be sited so that it is in a clear position on the deck and is easy to operate. The governing factors are the position of the chain locker and the alignment of the gipsy or warping drum with the hawse pipe or bow (stem-head) rollers.

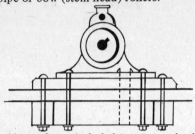

Fig. 44. Anchor winch bolting down detail

The holding down bolts should, if possible, be arranged to fit through the deck beams or a pad joggled over the beams and through fastened (*Fig. 44*). If needed, there should be a pad, preferably teak, under the winch to line it up in the required position. The whole assembly should be bedded down to the deck, the bolts being set in mastic or other waterproofing compound.

How are sheet winches mounted?

There are sheet winches to suit every sort of load and sail. They carry an enormous load and should always be of good quality. These winches should always be fitted to be fair with the lead of the sheet or fitted with a block lead or eye to bring the sheet into line. Pads should always be fitted if possible and the winch should be through bolted.

It is good practice to bolt through a beam or carline, or, if the winch is on a coaming side, this should be adequately strengthened with knees or gussets with particular attention being paid to the stress allied with the angle of load. The sizes of fastenings should be worked out in conjunction with the working load of the sail.

What materials are usually used for making hatches and skylights?

Teak is the best material with Cuban or Honduras mahogany next, followed by iroko. The joints are best glued with resorcinol glue but a urea formaldehyde type may also be used to advantage as it does not stain the exposed surfaces.

Which joints are usually used in hatch and skylight construction?

For corners the checked dovetail is the joint par excellence (*Fig. 45a*). Halving joints can also be used but are not as strong (see *Fig. 51*).

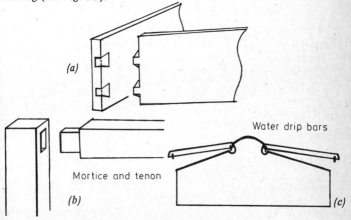

Fig. 45. Joints and skylight details. (a) Checked dovetail. (b) Mortice and tenon. (c) Skylight water drip bars

Hatch tops are usually panelled with the outer frame morticed and tenoned together (*Fig. 45b*). Watertightness is the main objective and the design and construction must be first class to attain this.

Hatch and skylight details are shown in *Fig. 45c*.

How are hatches, etc fastened to the deck?

There should be carlines and beams in way of the fixings as per *Fig. 46*.

Fig. 46. Hatch to carline bolting arrangement

What is a Dorade box and how is it made?

This is a type of waterproof ventilator and is usually used with a cowl-type ventilator. Although there is no reason why it should not be used with mushroom or other vents.

Fig. 47. A Dorade ventilator

The box can be made up as shown in *Fig. 47*. The deck fitting should be the same size as the cowl fitting and should stand proud of the deck by about 2 in to be effective. If light is needed below, the box can be fitted with a transparent top.

How is a rudder constructed?

A large rudder not capable of being cut from one board must be made up of pieces jointed together. This can be done by shaping and cutting the rudder blade, then the mating edges are rebated and fitted with a tongue, then glued together. The blade may then be drilled right through and held together with long rod fastenings clenched over at the ends.

Another method is to fit plates recessed into the blades. Sometimes it is possible for these plates to form the ends of the pintle or bearing straps. (*Fig. 48*).

The rudder stock is fitted with cheeks which run above the blade piece so that the top may be stopped off leaving a square recess for a tiller to be fitted.

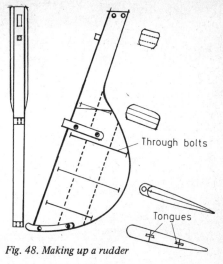

Through bolts

Tongues

Fig. 48. Making up a rudder

Which timbers are suitable for making tillers?

Nowadays it is quite usual to make laminated tillers, sometimes of contrasting woods to give an attractive appearance. Oak, hickory or rock elm are good timbers. Ash, teak and mahogany are also used occasionally.

How is laminating carried out?

Usually on a floor or board on which the curve required is laid out with blocks or shapes fastened down to allow the laminations to be cramped into shape whilst glueing. This is a very good method of making strong members for structural parts. When laminating, it is important that a good waterproof glue is used and that the laminations are not planed smooth on the glueing faces.

8

INTERIOR WORK

What are the important points to consider when panelling the inside of the hull?

The first consideration is the type of panelling and the ventilation to the hull. No panelling should ever seal a wooden hull entirely. There should be a good air gap at the top, and the bottom if possible should be left open to the bilge so that no part of the vessel contains dead air. It is also better if the panelling can be fixed to chocks or similar and not directly to the frames.

The inside of the hull and the back of the panelling should be painted with a primer and possibly a flexible oil-based (Danboline) paint.

Which materials are used for panelling and how are they fitted?

One of the most attractive types of panelling is battens of mahogany or teak varnished and screwed up with a gap of about 1½ in between them, these battens being about 2 in wide by ½ or ¾ in thick. If fastened with chrome screws and cups, they look attractive and not only provide ventilation but are easy to remove for hull maintenance.

Thin plywood is often used. This must be battened at the joints, which does not improve its appearance. Plywood should be to BS 1088, otherwise it will quickly delaminate.

Tongued and grooved matching is also occasionally used. If fitted well this makes a good job but needs to be of very thoroughly seasoned timber if it is not to show unsightly seams.

How are floorboard (cabin sole) supports fitted?

These must be made of fairly heavy material so that the sole does not flex. The ends should be half-jointed around the frames or timbers, stringers, etc. They should not rest on the planking (*Fig. 49a*).

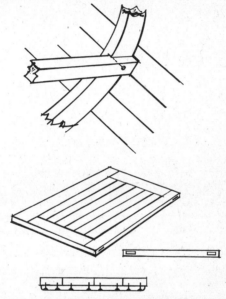

Fig. 49. The cabin sole. (a) Cabin floor support detail. (b) Types of floorboard

How should the floorboards be made up?

These can, of course, be ordinary straight laid planks but this always poses the problem of lifting for bilge access.

It is better to make the centre sections up into hatches that are easy to lift (*Fig. 49b*).

What is the method of making a pattern of the hull shape for fittings such as bulkheads, bunks etc?

This is done by spiling, i.e. a pattern is cut to fit roughly out of any suitable material such as hardboard. A small block of wood or calipers can be used to spile off on the pattern (*Fig. 50*). Move the wood spile or block along the surface marking off on the pattern with pencil or marker as this is done.

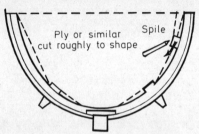

Fig. 50. Spiling a bulkhead shape

Another method is to mark off the pattern at regular or frequent intervals with dividers or calipers. This will enable an accurate shape to be marked out on the bulkhead or other member by adding on the thickness of the spile, e.g. 2 in if the block or batten is 2 in wide.

Yet another method is to simply mark off by measuring with a rule at intervals and joining these marks together.

How is the joinery work fitted together?

The various joints are shown in *Fig. 51*.

How are dry mattresses ensured?

A good method is to use 4 in wide battens spaced 2 in apart; this will give both ventilation and good support. It is possible to use webbing, such as is made by Pirelli, but this poses the problem of stiffening up the bunkboards sufficiently to take the sideways pull.

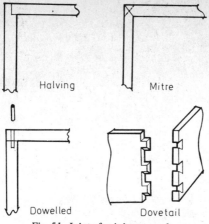

Halving

Mitre

Dowelled

Dovetail

Fig. 51. Joints for joinery work

Can a table be fitted that has drop leaves and provides both deck support and handholds?

The table shown in *Fig. 52* provides for these.

How wide should bookshelves be made and how can they be fiddled?

Books come in a vast number of sizes; some navigational books are quite large, i.e. 10 in high and 8 in deep, so these dimensions must be allowed for.

Fiddles are subject to much innovation. *Fig. 53* provides some ideas.

What are the important factors when fitting out the galley?

The three main factors are as follows:

    (a) The height and accessibility of the cooker and sink unit.

    (b) Stowage of cooker fuel, i.e. gas cylinders.

    (c) Safety, e.g. cooker fiddles, gimbals, etc.

The cooker must be placed in a well-ventilated position but free from draughts. It must be firmly fixed down. If it is a gas

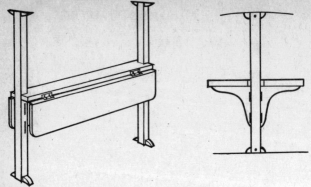

Fig. 52. A cabin table

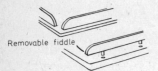

Removable fiddle

Fig. 53. Fiddles

Fig. 54. Gas cylinder stowage and drainage

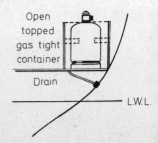

Open topped gas tight container

Drain

L.W.L.

cooker, the piping should be of solid drawn copper pipe through-out, with the exception of a gimballed type of cooker which must have an armoured flexible connection to the cooker.

There are many schools of thought attached to the stowage of the gas cylinder. By far the safest is to have the cylinder either outside on deck strapped down or in a drain-ventilated compartment (*Fig. 54*).

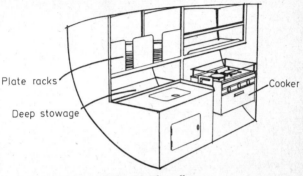

Fig. 55. The galley

Simple gimbals can be made up for most cookers. It is most important to find the centre of gravity first. Fiddles, if not already fitted, can be simply made up of stainless steel bar or rod (*Fig. 55*).

What are the requirements of the toilet compartment?

If it is a small boat it is sometimes awkward to fit a separate toilet compartment. There really is no substitute without inconvenience to the crew, so that every effort should be made to make enough space to install a sensible compromise.

Toilets come in many types and sizes. The traditional type works best and is the most robust.

If it is possible to fit a shower tray, this can serve the very useful purpose of doubling as an oilskin draining locker.

How are the thwarts fitted in a dinghy?

Rowing thwarts are usually made of solid timber. A good guide is that in a boat of say 6 ft beam, they will need to be at least $\frac{7}{8}$ in thick and 8 in wide if in hardwood. Teak is, of course, the best material.

The thwarts should fit snugly to the boat's side, joggled around the frames if necessary. There must be a stringer or cleats for the seats or thwarts to rest on. The height must be carefully considered and the thwart fitted at a comfortable position. Knees are used to strengthen and tie the whole job together. These should be through fastened in every case.

How are dinghy floor boards made up?

These are usually of softwood of light scantling. The planks are cut to a pleasing curve following the line of the bilge at the outboard edge and straightening to the hog on the inboard edge.

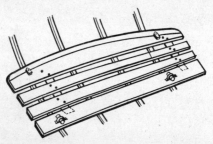

Fig. 56. Dinghy floor boards hog board fastening

They are usually fastened with copper nails or screws onto strips athwartships which are left slightly longer at the ends so that the sections can be cleated down by a hog board at the outside by turn-buckles (*Fig 56*).

9

MAINTENANCE

What maintenance is required?

The conscientious and vigilant owner will keep a notebook in which is entered anything which needs repair or overhaul in order of priority.

Maintenance includes painting and varnishing, curing leaks in the hull superstructure and deck. Skin fittings, stern gear and rudder bearings need checking, glands adjusting, etc. Rigging must be overhauled as must running gear, and if the boat has an auxiliary motor or motors, these must be maintained as well.

How is the topsides painting schedule carried out?

All painting, if the boat is not under cover, should be carried out in warm, dry and windless conditions.

If the paint is in good condition, a good rub down with wet or dry paper or pumice stone, used wet, may suffice to break the gloss. It is most important that the gloss is completely flatted or broken down to provide a good key for subsequent coating. In doing this it is possible that some of the seam stopping may show, and any high spots must be cleaned down to bare wood. Each place or spot where this occurs must be made good from the primer until the original stage is reached.

The whole surface is then undercoated. When this is dry it must be given a light rub down. Two undercoats are better than one. The paint should be brushed on in one direction and laid off in the other. It is important that a good finish is attained with each coat.

If a hull is paintsick, or the paint is peeling off because it is too thick, then it must be removed with either paint remover or burnt off with a blowlamp.

Burning off is the most effective. Care is needed so that the timber is not scorched, the paint heated only enough to make it lift easily with the stripping knife. Scorching destroys the surface and damages the wood, it also provides a barrier against good paint adhesion.

The seam and fastening stoppings should be carefully inspected at this point. Indeed, it is the ideal time to survey the whole of the timber of the hull. Any loose stopping should be raked out, the caulking inspected and hardened up if necessary, then restopped. Resinous knots should be primed with knotting. If using synthetic stoppers, these must be applied at this stage.

The hull is then thoroughly sanded down — by hand or with an orbital sander, and not with a disc as this will cause marks which would be extremely difficult to remove. A coat of priming should be applied to the surface.

When the primer is dry and hard is the time to cement-fill any imperfections, if using an ordinary oil-bound filler or trowel cement.

A further coat of primer is applied and when dry, three undercoats, rubbing down lightly between each coat. The undercoats should be well brushed out and laid off vertically or horizontally as required. This should be followed by the topcoat of enamel, which is fully applied, laid off and finished horizontally with good long brush-strokes. Good protection needs at least two finishing coats.

What does successful varnishing entail?

Conditions for successful varnishing must be ideal, i.e. warm and dry, windless and with the sun not too hot. All varnishing should be finished in time to set off before sunset or the evening dew, which would cause it to bloom.

If the timber shows any signs of blackness through the existing varnish, it may well be damp and it is best to scrape right down to bare wood, then leave it to dry out thoroughly. It is sometimes possible to bleach out stains or dark patches with oxalic acid crystals.

When the wood is dry it should be sanded down to a smooth finish and then wiped over either with a tack rag or a cloth soaked in white spirit. A coat of 50/50 varnish and white spirit or turpentine substitute is then applied and allowed to dry.

Each subsequent coat of varnish must be allowed to dry thoroughly before being rubbed down. Five coats of varnish would only be just enough for a good finish.

Rubbing down with steel wool or 400 grade wet and dry with white spirit will give a superb finish to the final coat. In outside conditions conventional varnish would appear to be of superior durability to polyurethane varnish, probably because it is more flexible and is not so likely to crack at the joints.

What is the sequence for painting below the waterline?

From the bare hull, the basic routine is the same as for the topsides except that the undercoats should be of the correct type to be compatible with the type of antifouling to be used.

Antifouling should never be burnt off as it gives off toxic fumes.

When scraping or sanding, goggles and a mask should be worn. Good ventilation is very necessary during application of antifouling paints.

Which are the special points below the waterline which may need maintenance?

(a) The rudder pintle bearings or hangings should be carefully inspected for corrosion and wear. If wear is allowed on these fittings it will rapidly worsen in use because the rudder and its fittings are subject to high stresses and continual movement (*Fig. 57*).

69

(b) Skin fittings, valves and cocks for toilets, cockpit drains, engine inlets, etc should be checked and tested, and glands repacked if necessary. The bolts and fastenings should be checked for soundness.

(c) The garboard seam, between the garboard strake and the keel, is the most likely seam to develop leaks and therefore the stopping should be carefully checked. If

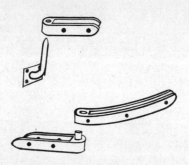

Fig. 57. Rudder pintles

there is any sign of movement or leakage the seam must be cleared of stopping and the caulking hardened up throughout its length.

What is the method for stopping seams?

It is seldom successful to try to caulk a part of a seam, as driving the caulking in any one place only tends to open the seam in another.

Stopping should not be plain putty, which is not waterproof. A good mixture can be made up of white lead putty with a small amount of red lead powder thoroughly mixed in; this can be let down very slightly with a little tallow which will make the mixture much more easily worked.

The seams should be primed before the stopping is applied.

70

What are the characteristics and uses of antifouling paints?

(a) There are numerous types of antifouling paints and coatings in the following principal forms. The first group is known as *'soft' antifouling*, i.e. the base is oil with cuprous arsenical or mercurial additives. This type sets up a reaction which forms a poisonous layer or area around the hull, thus preventing any living organisms from existing in its proximity. This type of antifouling gradually leaches away leaving only the base materials. This base usually scrubs off easily leaving the hull ready for re-coating.

(b) *Hard antifoulings* of the older type were usually of cellulose base with a high copper content. A great deal of trouble has been encountered with some types which have been found to cause electrolysis. Therefore it is of the utmost importance to use an antifouling which is compatible with the fastenings and fittings.

(c) *Plastic antifoulings.* These newer types of antifoulings have a number of advantages over the older types. Firstly they are claimed not to contain mercury and do not pollute the water. They are very easy to apply and have less toxic ingredients. Having a hard base they can be scrubbed regularly without detriment. It is also not necessary to immerse shortly after application, as with soft antifoulings, to retain the toxicity.

What precautions should be observed when applying antifouling paints?

Most antifouling paints are equally toxic to the operators and to the organisms which they are designed to deter. With this in mind, it is very important to read the maker's instructions.

Generally speaking, no smoking during application should be allowed. Protective or old clothing should be worn. Wearing gloves pays dividends, as these materials are difficult to remove and contain substances which are injurious to the skin. The eyes should be protected with goggles as these paints contain chemicals which can permanently damage the eyes.

71

DECAY AND BORERS

Which are the borers to be found in boats' timbers and how are they recognised?

The Gribble (*Limnoria lignorum*). A very common pest which is usually about $\frac{1}{5}$ in in length. It bores a tunnel a short distance into the timber. In a severe concentration these minute creatures will do much damage. Harbour piles and piers are frequently found to be completely eaten away. Fortunately painted or protected surfaces are immune from attack, as is teak.

If a small area is found to be affected on the surface of the planking or keel, it may be possible to burn the gribble out with a blowlamp then fill with a synthetic stopper. More extensive areas of damage will have to be cut away and a new section or graving piece fitted.

Teredo. A comparative newcomer to British waters, but found in warmer tropical waters everywhere, this mollusc has a very efficient boring mechanism resembling a tunnelling machine. As with the gribble, it does not attack a well-painted surface. Teak is seldom affected. In previous times, ships were sheathed with copper to prevent its entry. There are now other equally effective plastic sheathing materials available. The simple expedient of keeping plenty of paint on the underwater surfaces will do much to prevent the pest from obtaining entry.

What is the treatment for dry rot?

There are several types of dry rot, the most virulent is *Merulius lacrymens*. This is a fungus that feeds upon the cellulose content of the timber, eating it away until only crumbling dust remains; it is very fast working and spreading. Given the right conditions, a boat can be completely infected in a matter of months. There is no real cure for dry rot, other than cutting out the infected part or plank and burning it.

It is necessary to cut back at least two feet beyond any sign of decay or fungus in the timber. The whole of the area should be doused with Cuprinol or similar wood preservative.

What causes dry rot?

Dry rot only occurs where the conditions are suitable, i.e. moist, humid or warm damp situations especially where the situation is lacking in ventilation. All parts of a boat should be well ventilated to prevent rot commencing.

What is wet rot and what is its cause?

This condition is in fact not a true rot, it is usually caused by a high concentration of saturation. The wood often hardens considerably on drying.

If it is only a small or confined part of a member, such as a knee or part of a deadwood, after drying it may be possible to re-nature the timber by applying one of the modern capillary action epoxy solutions now available. Serious cases must, of course, be cut out and renewed.

How and why does electrolysis occur, and what can be done to prevent it?

This common fault can be caused by a great number of factors, e.g. an electrical fault finding its way to earth through the hull or fastenings or incompatible materials such as an iron rudder and a bronze propeller.

Wood affected by electrolysis becomes fibrous and denatured around fastenings and skin fittings. The only cure, if the trouble is caused by an electrical fault, is to check through the system and obviate the trouble at source. If, however, it is caused by incompatible materials such as an iron and copper mixture, one or other of the materials should be changed.

It may be necessary to obtain expert advice and consider anodic protection. Small uncomplicated problems, such as an iron rudder, may be cured by simply fitting zinc sacrificial plates.

APPENDIX 1

TIMBERS

Which are the recognised timbers most used in wooden boat construction?

Teak, mahogany, iroko, English elm, Rock elm, ash, oak, pitch pine, larch, cedar, spruce, Columbian pine, plywoods.

What are the characteristics and uses of these timbers?

Teak (Burma).   The colour ranges from golden brown through to very dark brown, and has a weight of about 40 to 45 lb per cubic foot when seasoned. Teak is extremely durable and is almost totally unaffected by rot or boring insects. It has a resin content which gives it an oily feel and has a strong characteristic smell when cut or worked. The water absorption rate is very low. It is comparatively easy to work but tools lose their edge rapidly and require frequent sharpening. It does not hold fastenings particularly well and needs to be carefully drilled for fastenings and fittings to prevent splitting.

Teak can prove difficult to glue satisfactorily, and great care in preparation when varnishing is necessary. It is the best material for planking, decking, hatches, skylights, coamings and general joinery work.

Mahogany.   There are many varieties of this wood, from many parts of the world. Most are pink or red in colour.

Cuban and Honduras mahoganies are by far the best but are difficult to obtain. They are extremely durable, and weigh about 33 to 35 lb per cubic foot when seasoned. The grain of mahogany is generally straight, it is easy to work, possesses great beauty when polished or varnished, holds fastenings well and has a low water absorption rate. It is very suitable for planking, hatches, coamings and joinery work.

Mahogany should not be used with iron fastenings, as this causes decay.

African mahogany. There are a number of so-called mahoganies each bearing a different name depending on the district of origin. They are hardwoods, and on average weigh about 36 lb per cubic foot when seasoned. The durability is fair, fastenings hold well, and they are compatible with most adhesives. Water absorption rate varies considerably in the various types, as does the colour which may range from very pale pink to quite dark red.

Most of these woods are difficult to work to a good finish because of their variable grain, which has a tendency to ruck up when planed. These timbers are widely used in moderate or low-priced construction.

Luan, or Philippine mahogany. This is a pinkish red coloured wood, a little heavier than the African mahoganies and similar in durability and working characteristics. It holds fastenings well and is satisfactory with most adhesives.

Fairly low in price and easy to obtain, it is useful for planking and general work if carefully selected.

Iroko. A hardwood, seasoned weight about 44 to 48 lb per cubic foot, brown or golden in colour. It is very durable, hard and close grained with a tendency to be difficult to work to a good finish. Its holding power with fastenings is first class and it has a good performance with most adhesives.

Iroko is available in large boards and is a good timber for planking and decking. It can be used for stems, keels and transoms.

75

English elm. A hardwood, native to the British Isles, it has a colour that ranges from golden brown to purple. The grain is very irregular. It possesses great strength and is comparatively heavy at 35 to 40 lb per cubic foot when seasoned.

This timber winds and distorts badly whilst laying for seasoning unless precautions are taken. It is also very prone to shakes and faults.

English Elm is only considered to be durable when used immersed in salt water. Traditionally it was widely used for keels, deadwood and planking below the waterline. Many dinghies are completely planked with elm.

Rock elm. This is a hardwood indigenous to North America and is usually known as Canadian Rock elm. When seasoned, its weight should be in the region of 44 lb per cubic foot.

It is a pale mauve brown colour with a consistent straight grain, considered to be very durable and has a low water absorption rate. Rock elm is one of the most flexible of all woods and can be steam bent to tight bends which makes it an excellent wood for steamed timbers and bent frames. It can also be used for keels and other structural members, is moderately easy to work and holds fastenings well.

Ash. A hardwood which grows in Britain. It is a heavy timber at about 43 to 46 lb per cubic foot when seasoned. Ash has a very straight grain and is extremely flexible and steams well. Unfortunately ash is of poor durability and suffers from a peculiar surface decay when exposed to wet conditions.

It works easily and holds fastenings well. If used in boat-building it should be well protected with paint or varnish.

English oak. This is the original village-square tree, a hard-wood that lives to a great age and is probably the most versatile of all timbers. It is heavy and, when seasoned, averages 48 to 52 lb per cubic foot. English oak, throughout the tree, consists of straight grained, bent and twisted grain, fibrous crooks and curves. It is extremely strong, hard and tough and has an oxalic acid content which produces a peculiar vinegary smell when it is cut or worked. It is a very durable timber, but will develop shakes and splits if left in open, unprotected situations. It ranges in colour from white to dark grey tinged with pink and it often has very beautiful figuring of the grain.

Oak quickly stains to purple or black when iron fastenings are used. It can be used for all structural parts of a boat, and can be steam bent well when young.

The bends and crooks, with careful selection, can be used for knees, breast hooks and stems etc. Its holding of fastenings is generally excellent.

Tools need to be kept very sharp to work oak satisfactorily.

Pitch pine.　　This timber comes from the southern United States. It is fairly heavy at 46 lb per cubic foot, contains much resin and is extremely durable. Pitch pine is very strong and supple and holds fastenings well. It needs very thorough preparation before painting to ensure that the resin is sealed. It is the best of all pines for decking and planking, but has now become difficult to obtain in the UK.

European larch.　　This is a deciduous conifer or softwood which is fast growing. Scottish larch is often considered to be the best. It is capable of producing long straight boards. The grain is straight, even and strongly pronounced.

The seasoned weight is approximately 36 lb per cubic foot. Its durability is rated as fair and it is strong and supple. The colour ranges from yellow to pink to dark brown. Careful drilling and fitting of fastenings is required to avoid splitting at hood ends etc. Larch is a popular choice of timber for planking and is much used in fishing boat construction.

Cedar.　　Honduras, or pencil cedar is a brown wood with a high durability rating. Because of its colour and appearance it is often mistaken for mahogany, but is much lighter at approximately 28 to 30 lb per cubic foot, seasoned.

Cedar has a straight grain and is fairly strong but because of its soft texture it can be easily bruised or crushed.

It is easy to work and has a pleasant sweet smell, hence its use for making cigar boxes.

A good planking timber for light craft such as class racing yachts and motorboats, cedar was much used in former times for joinery work in large racing yachts.

Port Orford cedar. A much softer wood which is lighter in weight, generally speaking, than Honduras or pencil cedar, it is usually brown with a pink tinge. Durability is good and it can be used for planking.

Columbian pine. This is a softwood of medium durability. It has a strongly pronounced grain and is supple and strong. Its weight, when seasoned, is usually 30 to 33 lb per cubic foot. Columbian pine is sometimes mistaken for pitch pine, but it lacks the resinous content of this wood. It can be used for planking and decking and masts and spars of solid construction, but its high moisture absorption rate and shrinkage in dry conditions give it poor caulking watertightness characteristics.

Norway spruce. A conifer and the traditional Christmas tree. When cut, it is sold as deal. It is a fairly durable timber with a seasoned weight of about 32 lb per cubic foot.

A good timber for solid masts or spars of fairly small scantling, Norway spruce is not often used for planking except for tongued and grooved decking that is to be covered with painted canvas, etc. This type of deck has, in any case, been largely superseded by the use of plywood for this purpose. Deal is easy to work and is liable to split unless carefully fastened. If used for planking it should be thoroughly protected with paint.

Sitka or silver spruce.   This is a softwood of the conifer family, at this time the most heavily planted tree in the British Isles.

Sitka spruce is very light at 25 to 28 lb per cubic foot when seasoned. It is much valued for masts and spars of both solid and hollow construction, also for planking small craft. Racing skiff oars are traditionally made of spruce.

. It is silvery pink in colour, and has an attractive sheen when planed. The durability is good, but it should always be well protected with varnish or paint as the water absorption rate tends to be high. Care should be taken when fastening not to crush the fibres because of its soft texture. It is available in fairly wide boards.

Kauri pine.   This is a New Zealand softwood of moderate durability with a seasoned weight of approximately 35 lb per cubic foot. Kauri pine has a close straight grain, is easily worked and holds fastenings well. It was a favoured timber for decking in the days of the 'J' class yachts. Like many other pines, it is now difficult to obtain. It can be used for planking or decking.

Plywood.   Marine ply is usually made up of mahogany veneers in a variety of thicknesses and sizes. Ply for marine use must comply with BS 1088 or 4907.

This material needs very careful selection to obtain the best quality. It is a very useful material for building yacht tenders and racing dinghies, also for bulkheads and joinery.

What are the defects likely to be found in timber (when selecting)?

Mahoganies.   Rot shows up as a dead looking white area. Lightning shakes, transverse shakes across the grain, are quite difficult to detect. They are usually caused by bad felling (*Fig. 58a*). Other faults include star shakes and cup shakes.

Elm.   Soft spots of rot are usually grey in colour in contrast to the surrounding wood. Shakes and longitudinal splits often occur.

Oak.   Rot shows up as a blotchy area of dead looking material, paler in colour than the surrounding sound wood. Oak is also liable to have numerous shakes if it has been seasoned too quickly. Small shakes are of little detriment but star shakes radiating from the heart wood should be suspect (*Fig. 58b*).

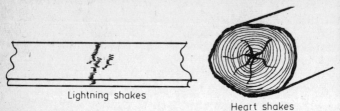

Lightning shakes

Heart shakes

Fig. 58. Faults in timber. (a) Lightning shake or upset. (b) Star shakes

Softwoods.   Generally rot or decay shows up as a grey blotchy looking area.

What are the ways of seasoning timber?

There are many ways of seasoning timber, both artificially and naturally. Natural seasoning is always considered to be the best but takes a long time.

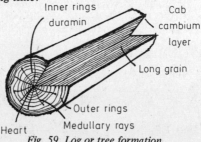

Inner rings

duramin

Cab

cambium

layer

Long grain

Outer rings

Medullary rays

Heart

Fig. 59. Log or tree formation

Timber should be cut or felled when the sap is at rest, i.e. during the winter months (*Fig. 59*). Softwood trees are felled, barked, logged and then the sapwood is removed, leaving a square section. These are called deals or baulks. These baulks are stacked in criss-cross fashion so that the air will circulate between them and they will season naturally. First grade wood is usually seasoned under cover. This process takes from 3 to 6 months. *Fig. 60a* shows the conversion of softwoods.

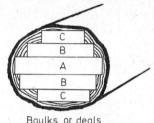

Baulks or deals

Fig. 60. (a) Conversion of softwood

Wet seasoning is a process used in the USA and Canada. This involves leaving the logs in running water with the ends of the logs facing upstream. This washes out the sap and in turn puts in a high water content which is easily removed.

Kiln dried or seasoned wood is produced by putting the wood into a kiln, cross lagged, and hot air at about $92\,^{\circ}C$ is circulated for one to two weeks.

Hardwood seasoning takes about three times as long as softwood and, with very hard wood, may take as long as one month to every inch of diameter. The conversion of hardwoods is usually done by sawing along the length of the log, making it into planks. These are stacked or logged with approximately ½ in battens between each plank. *Fig. 60b* shows the principal methods of conversion relating to hardwoods.

The selection of the correct cut of timber for the various parts of construction is important. Generally speaking, tangential cut timber is used for planking, sheerstrakes, coamings, coachroof sides, cabin sole boards, tongued and grooved boards for bulkheads or deck which are to be covered and general joinery work.

Tangential cut boards have a greater moisture absorption rate on the exposed face than rift cut, and because of the tendency to bow up or down across the board should be kept fairly narrow if used for general work such as planking.

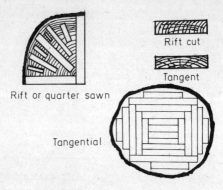

Rift cut

Tangent

Rift or quarter sawn

Tangential

Fig. 60. (b) Conversion of hardwood

Rift cut is used for laid decks, covering boards and hand-rails because it does not wear down between the grain and become splinter prone. It also bends more readily for curved plank decking.

Bent frames should have the grain across the frame to facilitate bending.

APPENDIX 2

FASTENINGS AND ADHESIVES

Fastenings

Most sizes of fastenings are available from stock but it may be necessary to have large bolts of any material made up specially for the job.

Copper boat nails

These are readily available from stock and are usually sold by weight. The gauge indicates the size and the numbers go in reverse, i.e. 16 gauge is the smaller and 6 the bigger.

They are available in a large variety of lengths from ½ in to 6 in or larger.

Roves are also sold by weight and these are measured by the diameter in inches, i.e. a number 6 nail has a ¾ in rove.

Copper boat nails can be used as a straight nail fastening, turned or clenched over a rove.

Holes for copper nails should always be pre-drilled, the hole being approximately half of the diagonal if used in hardwood and half of the diameter or plat if used in softwood. There should always be a small countersunk recess to take the head. In carvel construction this would be a counterbore which can be stopped or dowelled.

Ring barbed nails

These are available in both silicon bronze and monel. Correctly used, they have good holding capability but if drawn cannot be re-driven in the same hole and the next size nail must be used. These nails cannot be turned or clenched as they are hard and would break.

They are available in many gauges. The thinner type is very useful for glued and nailed construction, e.g. in plywood boat building.

Cut nails or dumps

These are of iron and are difficult to obtain nowadays. They are used in commercial or fishing boat construction and provide great holding power when driven into hardwood. It is necessary to drill and counterbore for these fastenings. Sometimes steel galvanised dumps are available; if driven into oak or teak the galvanising is quickly leached away, leaving ordinary steel which is a most unsuitable material for boat fastenings.

Panel pins

Available in quite a few sizes, useful for holding together glued construction but have neither holding power nor durability.

Brass ovals

These are sometimes to be found and are useful for inside joinery, etc where there is no water to leach out the zinc content of the brass. These nails can usually be driven without drilling and can be punched under flush, leaving only a very small hole.

Screws

These are the most versatile of all fastenings and come in a large variety of sizes and gauges. Brass screws should not be used as they quickly dezincify and disintegrate. Silicon bronze, aluminium bronze, gunmetal, stainless steel and monel are satisfactory materials and are fairly easy to obtain. Galvanised steel screws are also used, but the zinc coating must be hot dipped and not zinc plated. Galvanised screws call for extreme care when driving as the coating is easily damaged at the slot.

Screw sizes are calibrated in gauges ranging from the smaller 4 or 6 up to 28 or so.

Screws must always be drilled for; the diameter of the head plus is the counterbore size, the diameter of the shank should be carried through the plank or part that is being fastened, and 2/3 of the root size drilled into the frame etc.

A small smear of tallow helps driving and it is important that the screwdriver or bit is a proper fit in the slot. Do not expect a screwdriver that is suitable for a No. 8 screw to be any use for a No. 16.

Bolts and nuts

These are readily available in all metals, although the larger sizes may need making to order. Silicon bronze or stainless are the best but galvanised types are widely used. Do not use glavanised bolts with teak. Iron bolts dipped in Stockholm tar are first class fastenings for heavy work boat construction.

Bolts must always be fitted in a neat size hole and a washer used under the nut with compound and cotton to achieve a waterproof joint.

Adhesives

Modern developments in synthetic adhesives have revolutionised the wooden boat building industry.

Recommendations have been drawn up by The Ship and Boat Builders National Federation and The Timber Research and Development Association who state that only synthetic resin glues should be used in the construction of marine craft. These must comply with BS 1204 Type M.R. (moisture resistant, gap filling) or BS 1204 W.B.P. (weather and boil proof). Glues must be gap filling as laid down in BS 1204. The main types are:

(a) *Urea formaldehyde resin.* BS/1204/MR water resistant to cold water immersion but not weatherproof, limited durability, suitable for dinghies and joinery work.

85

(b) *Resorcinol resin*. BS/1204/WBP weatherproof, durable and suitable for all types of work.

With urea formaldehyde and phenol formaldehyde glues the moisture content of the timber should be 12% to 15%. With resorcinol this should be 15% to 18%. However, there is no accurate way of determining moisture content apart from a meter, though a rough estimate can be got by weight per cubic foot. The only sure way is strict storage humidity control.

Epoxy resin is also a very useful glue for a number of applications in the marine industry. This type of glue is available in many consistencies and setting times and can be used with all types of timber. It has a number of advantages over resorcinol glues, one important factor is that it does not give off toxic fumes when used in a confined space. Another is that it is light in colour, some grades are clear, thus there is no staining of the timber.

Setting times may range from about 5 minutes to 24 hours. This factor can be used to advantage with various applications. Cramping time can be short enabling the job to progress more quickly than with the use of other types of adhesive.

GLOSSARY

Apron   The member at the inside of the stem to which the plank ends are fastened.

Beam   A structural member fixed transversely supporting the deck.

Bearding   The line at the back of the stem or apron where the planking leaves contact.

Breast hook   A type of knee which strengthens the bow.

Buttock   A line on the hull plan drawn parallel to the centre line or keel.

Canoe stern   Vessel with curved sternpost where the planks come together.

Carline   A fore-and-aft beam supporting a hatch or other deck fitting, and the inner ends of the beams.

Caulking   Cotton, oakum or compound which is used in the seams.

Clench   To rivet up the inner end of a nail or fastening over a rove or washer.

Clencher or clinker   A method of construction whereby the planks overlap each other giving a stepped or joggled appearance.

Coaming   An edge piece or plank of the cockpit or similar which stands up to prevent the ingress of water.

Cruiser stern   Where there is an almost vertical or forward raked sternpost and which the planking meets.

Deadwood   Timber fitted between the keel and sternpost or stem. Sometimes loosely used to mean keel rubber or filling piece.

Dump   A metal nail of the cut or tapered type used in low price construction.

Fair off   To perfect the curvature of the hull lines or timbers so that they run true.

Fastening   Any type of fixing to hold members in place.

Floor   A main strengthening member fitted athwartships on top of the keel and tying the planking together.

Futtock   A frame or timber made up of several pieces.

Garboard seam   The seam between the garboard strake and the keel.

Garboard strake   The plank next to the keel.

Graving piece   A small piece of wood let in to repair damage.

Gribble   A marine borer which attacks unprotected timber.

Hog   The member fastened to the inside of the keel to take the fixing of the garboard strake.

Keel   The main backbone of the boat.

Keelson   A fore-and-aft member on top of the keel.

Knee   A strengthening member to strengthen or tie a corner together.

Land   The part of a plank which joins to the next in a clencher boat.

Lay off, to   To set out the plans in the mould loft.

Limber   A hole or gap between the hog and garboard under the floors and frames to let bilge water run.

Monel   An alloy used for fastenings, shafts etc.

Moulds   Shapes of the hull erected on the keel to govern the shape of the planking.

Navel pipe   A metal fitting through the deck for the anchor chain to stow through.

Oakum   Hemp teased out for caulking.

Offsets   A table of measurements complementary to the plans.

Partners   A wedged frame where the mast passes through the deck.

Pattern   A shape made up full size to act as a template for making a part.

Pay   To fill a seam with stopping.

Rebate   A groove in the stem, etc to take the ends of the planking.

Rocker   The curve on the bottom of a keel (fore and aft).

Scantling   The measurement or size of a structural member.

Scarf (or scarph)   A joint longitudinally in timber where the part continues at the same or similar size.

Sheerstrake   The top plank or strake on the hull.

Sided   The finished size or scantling of a keel or similar part.

Spile   To mark around, e.g. bulkheads, planks etc.

Shelf or clamp   The longitudinal member each side of the hull, inside, to carry the deck beams.

Step (mast)   A mortice in the keel or a block thereon to take the heel of the mast.

Stopwater   A transverse dowel fitted through the line of a joint or scarf in the stem or keel.

Tabernacle   A fitting for the mast when stepped on deck so that it may be lowered.

Thwart   A seat in a small boat, e.g. athwartships.

Timber   Usually refers to a steamed frame.

Tingle   A plate or patch on the planking.

Treenails   Wooden peg fastenings for planking, etc.

Truck   A round piece of wood to protect the end grain of a mast or ensign staff, also carries sheaves for light halyards.

Trunk (rudder)   Case or pipe through the hull to take the rudder stock.

Tuck   The concave shape of a boat's bottom where the planking curves towards stem or stern.

Washboards   Boards slotted into a cabin entrance instead of a door or loose planks in slots on decks of fishing boats.

Waterline   The level at which a boat rests in the water, or lines at regular spacing on plans enabling measurement for lofting etc to be taken off.

INDEX